Words around

ID0731971

Words around the Fire

REFLECTIONS ON THE SCRIPTURES OF THE EASTER VIGIL

by
Gail Ramshaw

Art by
Linda Ekstrom

Liturgy Training Publications

With gratitude to Gordon Lathrop

––––––––

Other books in this series:
Words around the Table
Words around the Font
Words That Sing (book and cassettes)

––––––––

The scripture readings contained herein are from the *Revised Standard Version Bible*,
copyright © 1946, 1952, 1971 by the Division of Christian Education
of the National Council of Churches of Christ in the U.S.A.,
as emended in the *Lectionary for the Christian People*,
copyright © 1988 by Pueblo Publishing Company, Inc.
Used with permission. All rights reserved.

Design by Jane Kremsreiter.

Copyright © 1990 Archdiocese of Chicago. All rights reserved.
Liturgy Training Publications
1800 North Hermitage Avenue
Chicago IL 60622-1101
1-800-933-1800
FAX 1-800-933-7094

ISBN 0-929650-14-X
WORDS
$6.95

Printed in the United States of America.

Contents

Foreword

FIRE LEAPS, starts, sparks, here, there, gold, black, a power for destruction without which human civilization would have no warmth or light. You cannot grasp it in your hand; you cannot survive without its mystery and might. And the fire is Christ.

The fire shines before and among us in the great Paschal Vigil. How to say the fire? How to say Christ? The biblical readings say something of God's mystery and might. But the words dart and quiver before the assembled church, words impossible to grasp, words essential for our survival. It is good to try to say what the fire is, Christ the Fire.

Here are meditations on the Easter Vigil's readings, attempts to say what the Fire is. There is considerable congruence in the appointed readings among the churches for this, the central Christian festival. This collection will comment upon the seven readings appointed in the Roman lectionary and refer to others found in the Episcopal, the Lutheran and the Common lectionaries. The readings themselves have been included here; each text follows the reflection.

It is my hope that these biblically inspired reflections will benefit the folk in all the churches who are celebrating again the ancient Queen of Liturgies.

Gail Ramshaw
FEAST OF ST. MARY MAGDALENE, 1989

IT IS SAID that in pre-Christian times the peasants of northern Europe would assemble on the hilltops in the springtime. There they would light enormous bonfires to alert Woden, the master of the sky, that winter had better be over. The people, weary of long nights and cold days, would gather around the fire as a sign of gathering around their divinity, and they would plead for the return of life.

We Christians have inherited this religious custom. Originally the light of the Easter Vigil was the table lamp lighted by the woman in the Jewish household. As Christians moved from house to basilica, the light grew and grew. We see the paschal candlestands in European cathedrals, ten, twenty feet tall, and smile at our mental image of robed men circling around such a phallic light. But during some century or another, perhaps after the demise of Woden, Christians adopted the pagan springtime ritual. They gathered in the light of spring's first full moon to strike the year's new light and to raise a bonfire as a sign of the life God brings.

Christ Our Light

Since prehistoric times fire has been viewed as a sign of divine presence and power. Greek myth, which knew nothing of divine grace, terrorized the people with the tale of Prometheus, who stole fire from the gods and gave it to the world's poor human beings, who were struggling for heat and light and food. The myth says that Zeus punished Prometheus by chaining him forever to the rock where eagles pecked at his liver. But the Hebrew tradition knew a God of mercy. The God of the covenant did not spitefully withhold fire from earthlings or punish its use. Yet fire remained a sign of divinity, a symbol of almighty power, as if each flame is a spark of God. The Hebrew Scriptures tell wondrous stories of God in the fire and of the faithful gathered around the fire as around God. Let us peer across the flickering gold of the blaze and see whom we recognize.

Genesis 3:24   There are Adam and Eve, banished from the garden, taking one last glance at the tree of life, their view blocked by the flaming swords of the cherubim. God's righteous fire cuts Adam and Eve off from paradise, and they flee from the divine power of the fire.

Exodus 3:1–12   There is Moses, gazing into the burning bush, hearing the divine voice and seeing a mysterious fire that does not burn. The fire enlightens Moses, and he sets off to lead the people to the promised land. The God in the fire of the bush ignited the people with the power of freedom.

Exodus 19:16–20   There are the throngs of Israel, assembled around Mount Sinai as it explodes with fire, cinders raining down into the crowd, smoke ascending back to heaven, this mighty sign of divinity beckoning to the refugees. Moses climbs up the mountain and somehow enters the fire to see God.

Exodus 13:21–22   There are the same Israelite throngs walking through the wilderness, living precariously with meager food and water, but graciously guarded and guided by the beneficent light of the pillar of fire. Each night they are blessed by the light of God, and the darkness does not overwhelm them.

1 Kings 6:14–22   There is Solomon at the temple. The light of Sinai and the pillar of fire have been captured and molded into the gold of the temple. The main temple doors open eastward, and so the morning sun brightens the temple precincts with divine benediction.

1 Kings 18:20–40   There, too, is Elijah on Mount Carmel for the great contest of the gods. Who is the god powerful enough to end this drought, Baal or the

LORD? As contemporary religious ritual dictated, each group of devotees builds an altar, lays on it a bull and entreats its god to send down divine fire, thus receiving the sacrifice into heaven. The prophets of Baal beg and plead, bewail and gesticulate, but from Baal no fire comes. Elijah prays for a sign from the LORD, and divine fire descends in a blinding flash, consuming the bull, the wood, the stone, the dust and the water in the trench. "The LORD is God" cry the people, assembled around the fire.

At the Easter Vigil the flame is a small one, nothing like these great burnings of divine presence. All heavenly conflagrations and all fiery signs of God are focused into the single flame of the candle around which we gather. Later, on Easter day, it is easy for Christian churches to sing the glories of the spring day, what with the sunshine, daffodils, lilies, hats and choirs cheerfully celebrating. But the Exsultet is sung long before the day's light. In the dark it quotes the psalm, "And the night is as clear as day." At the Vigil we laud, praise, glorify and honor a single flame as if that flame were the whole consuming fire of God. And as we gather around the fire, we chant the words, "Christ our light."

Religious paintings customarily have depicted Jesus in white robes, perhaps to signify his purity, perhaps to denote him in the crowd. Clever artists control the light in their paintings so that ever so subtlely Christ is the source of illumination. But the truth is that we see Christ in light, as light, as our light, only by faith. The magi followed a supernatural light to find a king, and they arrived to worship a common infant. The humorist Garrison Keillor, narrating the visit of the magi, *Matthew 2:9* commented, "Have you ever tried to follow a star? It means they went by faith." Neither the infant nor the adult Jesus wore white, radiated beams or emitted a halo. Jesus' life was enclosed by darkness, the night of his birth and the eclipse at his death. Those who see in Christ the light of God are illumined by faith. Early believers called baptism "illumination," for through faith the world, the renewed community and the self are seen anew in the light of God.

The scriptures present the mystery of the resurrection in several
ways. There is the news of the empty tomb. There are stories of angels' visitations and stories of appearances of the risen Lord. Luke's chronol-
ogy tells of appearances of Christ for 40 days and the bestowal of
Christ's spirit on the 50th day. Some of these appearances occur "eight days later," that is, when the followers of Jesus had assembled for weekly
prayers. Paul sees the risen one in a blinding light. All these—empty tomb, angels, appearances of Christ, the ascension, Pentecost, visions—are ways to narrate our faith that what we expect from death has been reversed by God in Christ. We expect a body to rot and human memory to fade. Instead, the spirit of Jesus gives life to the body of Christ throughout the world.

We begin the Vigil not with narratives of the resurrection but with a symbol of it: "Christ our light," we say. Darkness we know too well: the toddler's plea that the night-light be left on, the grandpa's terror that he might go blind, the growing depression of the community after days of gray rain or winter's early nightfall. Into such darkness threatening to overwhelm the world comes Christ our light, reversing human fact with divine truth.

When Luke narrates the bestowal of Christ's spirit, he describes
on the head of each disciple a tongue as of fire. A paschal flame dances on the head of each of the faithful, as if now, after the resurrection, the fire of God disperses within the community. "Christ our light," we chant. As we watch the candle flicker, not only do we remember the stories of the fire of God, but we also see Christ our light on one another gathered around the fire.

4

In the morning sun:
Christ, our light.

In the shining stars:
Christ, our light.

In the burning bush:
Christ, our light.

In the pillar of fire:
Christ, our light.

In the glistening temple:
Christ, our light.

In the tongues of flame:
Christ, our light.

AT A MIDWESTERN SEMINARY a professor of pastoral care assigns the seminarians to unearth the stories of their birth. What memories do your parents recall of how you came to be? Are there stories of the birth itself? How did you come to be so named? The professor and the students find that these stories may not be factually accurate, but through the words of the stories we hear the family's self-identity.

In my family of origin we have a chant: "When Kurt was three, Paul was born; when Paul was three, Gail was born; when Gail was SIX, the twins were born; when the twins were three, Elaine was born." Thus we attested to our devout conviction that God, knowing of the eventual arrival of twins, delayed that pregnancy for three years so that mother would be prepared for all the extra work of two babies. No doubt an astute family therapist would detect yet more in this family chant. To discover a family system, its bonds, its breaks, its values, its shame, listen to the birth stories.

Whole peoples have birth stories. The United States has two oft-repeated, mutually contradictory tales of its origin. In one, a noble

Genesis 1—2

band of pious English folk, like the holy people of Israel, pass over the sea to a new freedom centered in the worship of God. Here the values are religious, communal, ordained. In the other story, solitary adventurers and lone explorers from many different lands strike out for economic gain in a romantic search for private space. (Read the diaries and correspondence of the pioneer women who saw little on the prairie road but the graves of those who had gone before.) Here the values are secular, individualistic, practical. Daily life in the United States evokes both of these birth stories. After months of protecting our home on the range we each weary of the conquest of the West: then there comes a national holiday, such as Thanksgiving or Martin Luther King, Jr. Day, that makes us recall Plymouth Rock.

It was not from a Christian but from a Jew that I first heard that Genesis gives the faithful two birth stories. I had learned that there was only one story left, Genesis 3. This second story, the Fall, was written on top of the first in such forceful strokes that only it was legible. And so I learned in catechism, "Do you believe that you are a sinner? Yes, I believe that I am a sinner," and I dutifully recited this exercise to prepare for a lugubrious monthly observance of holy communion in our Lutheran congregation. But my Jewish friend said that the second story is only half the truth, that the first truth stands out in strength and joy in the consciousness of God's people: "And God saw everything that *Genesis 1:31* had been made, and behold, it was very good." At a recent elementary-school graduation the principal asserted that a central thesis that the curriculum seeks to inculcate is that we are good. And I thought with wistful ambivalence of my catechism, and of the changing moods of the decades, and I wondered whether the truths of goodness and of sin can ever come to live in honest, healthy tension, the two birth stories like bookends holding in the pages of our days.

In the Christian West the truth of the Fall has sunk like a dead weight into our imagination. It is not only because comedy relies so heavily on social convention and on vernacular wordplay that tragedy is longer lived and more deeply felt. It is rather that so many Western people find tragedy more exact than comedy, failure more familiar than success, loss more universal than happiness, the Inferno more believable than Paradise. Perhaps this is why the news reports daily of murder and sedition, betrayal and despair, as if the news is like the catechism with which we rehearse versions of that story deepest in our psyche, the birth story of Genesis 3.

All the more reason that Christians gather once a year at springtime, in the darkness of night to be sure, to revive in themselves the truth of Genesis 1. Here is a birth story astonishingly comic, in which everything turns out right in the end. This first story says God has conquered chaos, the universe is kindly and beautiful, the world is ordered expressly to serve humankind, humankind is created in the divine image, male and female are equal and perfect. There is even food aplenty without killing the animals. And there is such bounty in the world that one day in seven can be given over to rest.

Our experience is quite the opposite. Our days suggest life without God, months of chaos, a dying ecosystem, murderous peoples, centuries of sexism, unending toil, sin everywhere. So to proclaim the resurrection we read this first birth story in which the universe is splendidly created by a benevolent God and in which we women and men live side by side in the divine image. Out of chaos God brings beauty. Out of the watery mass God forms life. The Hebrew words for chaos are onomatopoeic, almost funny: *tohu-wabohu*, "without form and void." And we know what *tohu-wabohu* means when our spirits are as disordered as our bureau drawers. But God's Spirit hovers like a nesting bird (says the Hebrew verb) over the waters, the water of chaos and of our tears and of our baptism, and what is born is that primordial sign of divine life: light. Here is a birth story worth remembering: We are born out of watery chaos to rejoice in the light of God.

Genesis 1:2

Although we too quickly dismiss this beneficent account of our birth, the scriptures do not leave the story of creation in Genesis 1. Of course the ancient Hebrews saw that daily life did not mirror the

Genesis 3:7
Genesis 4:8
Genesis 3:18
peaceful order of the first creation story. The first family knows shame, and as soon as there are brothers there is fratricide. The earth brings forth thorns and thistles, and the social order knows more of thorns than of the fruited tree of life. But the last chapters of the book of Isaiah recall the first creation story: "Arise, shine, for your light has Isaiah 60–66 come!" Into a world covered with thick darkness will dawn a newly created light of God. Your family will be radiant and joyful, the animals of the universe will serve you, all the trees will offer wood for God's sanctuary. The new creation will be better than the first—the sun and the moon need no longer shine, for the glory of God will light the human race. Rather than fig leaves or animal skins, we will wear garments of salvation and robes of righteousness, dressed by God as for a wedding, for we will marry our God. Our potter God will mold us anew. No more will infants die; everyone will live a hundred years: The wolf and the lamb shall feed together. All shall be satisfied, nursed by the mothering universe and a mothering God. "For behold, I create new Isaiah 65:17 heavens and a new earth," says our God.

Lest we forget these birth stories of God's creation, the gospel of John 1:1–18 John heard on Christmas Day opens with the phrase, "In the beginning," and retells our gracious birth story. Here the creation story is told in the light of the word of God. This word is Christ, the light that the darkness cannot overcome. This light enlightens all the world. Here is our birth story: We are born again into the light of God. In this light we know ourselves to be the image of God, for we live in the one who is the image of God.

As the scriptures began with creation, so they conclude with creation. The visionary writes, "Then I saw a new heaven and a new Revelation 21:1—22:5 earth." All the dreams of Isaiah are to be realized, with the lamp of the Lamb as the glory of God fulfilling any need for sun and moon. The new earth is a perfected, symmetrical, bejeweled and gilded city housing all the peoples of the world. The river of life flows for all; the tree of life bears every created fruit, because the tree, like the river, is Christ. All of us who had only three drops of water on our forehead will, in this city, see shining on our foreheads through those meager but sufficient drops the name of God.

It is the Easter Vigil, and we gather to hear our birth story. The story is ours in common, for our birth from the waters of chaos binds us into one. Annually, as at a birthday party, we assemble around the candle and the font to answer the professor's questions. What memories are there of how you came to be? We read Genesis 1 aloud. Are there stories of the birth itself? We assemble at the font. How did you come to be so named? We are named children of God, for by the mystery of Easter we are granted this name whispered first at creation and heard more clearly at Christmas. This is our birth story, here is our name, and the family photo album is standing all around us.

IN THE BEGINNING God created the heavens and the earth. The earth was without form and void, and darkness was upon the face of the deep; and the Spirit of God was moving over the face of the waters.

And God said, "Let there be light"; and there was light. And God saw that the light was good; and God separated the light from the darkness. God called the light Day, and the darkness God called Night. And there was evening and there was morning, one day.

And God said, "Let there be a firmament in the midst of the waters, and let it separate the waters from the waters." And God made the firmament and separated the waters which were under the firmament from the waters which were above the firmament. And it was so. And God called the firmament Heaven. And there was evening and there was morning, a second day.

And God said, "Let the waters under the heavens be gathered together into one place, and let the dry land appear." And it was so. God called the dry land Earth, and the waters that were gathered together God called Seas. And God saw that it was good. And God said, "Let the earth put forth vegetation, plants yielding seed, and fruit trees bearing fruit in which is their seed, each according to its kind, upon the earth." And it was so. The earth brought forth vegetation, plants yielding seed according to their own kinds, and trees bearing fruit in which is their seed, each according to its kind. And God saw that it was good. And there was evening and there was morning, a third day.

And God said, "Let there be lights in the firmament of the heavens to separate the day from the night; and let them be for signs and for seasons and for days and years, and let them be lights in the firmament of the heavens to give light upon the earth." And it was so. And God made the two great lights, the greater light to rule the day, and the lesser light to rule the night; God made the stars also. And God set them in the firmament of the heavens to give light upon the earth, to rule over the day and over the night, and to separate the light from the darkness. And God saw that it was good. And there was evening and there was morning, a fourth day.

And God said, "Let the waters bring forth swarms of living creatures, and let birds fly above the earth across the firmament of the heavens." So God created the great sea monsters and every living creature that moves, with which the waters swarm, according to their kinds, and every winged bird according to its kind. And God saw that it was good. And God blessed them, saying, "Be fruitful and multiply and fill the waters in the seas, and let birds multiply on the earth." And there was evening and there was morning, a fifth day.

And God said, "Let the earth bring forth living creatures according to their kinds: cattle and creeping things and beasts of the earth according to their kinds." And it was so. And God made the beasts of the earth according to their kinds and the cattle according to their kinds, and everything that creeps upon the ground according to its kind. And God saw that it was good.

Then God said, "Let us make humankind in our image, after our likeness; and let them have dominion over the fish of the sea, and over the birds of the air, and over the cattle, and over all the earth, and over every creeping thing that creeps upon the earth." So God created humankind in the divine image; in the image of God humankind was created; male and female God created them. And God blessed them, and God said to them, "Be fruitful and multiply, and fill the earth and subdue it; and have dominion over the fish of the sea and over the birds of the air and over every living thing that moves upon the earth." And God said, "Behold, I have given you every plant yielding seed which is upon the face of all the earth, and every tree with seed in its fruit; you shall have them for food. And to every beast of the earth, and to every bird of the air, and to everything that creeps on the earth, everything that has the breath of life, I have given every green plant for food." And it was so. And God saw everything that had been made, and behold, it was very good. And there was evening and there was morning, a sixth day.

Thus the heavens and the earth were finished, and all the host of them. And on the seventh day God finished the work which had been done, and God rested on the seventh day from all the work which God had done.

O mother, O God,
your creation is very good:
the darkness of this church,
the light of your life,
our birth in these waters,
your image in us all.
O good mother, O God,
we rest in you.

THE TALES OF GOD'S PEOPLE include a number of call narratives. God calls the person by name, and the response is always, "Here am I." Abraham, Jacob, Moses, Samuel and Isaiah are called to change their lives or to perform a mission, to live anew in response to God. Thus it is not inappropriate that for many Christians their baptism day is also their public naming day. Not only are we baptized into the whole body of God's people to receive a communal identity, we also are called by name into a life of service unlived as yet by any other human being. Genesis 22 is one such call narrative. We join Abraham in answering the call, and we gather on Mount Moriah around the most enigmatic fire of all. No stereotypical sign of God's presence, this fire—if we take the text seriously—was meant for the sacrifice of Isaac.

Genesis 12:1
Genesis 28:13–15
Exodus 3:4
1 Samuel 3:4
Isaiah 6:8

The story of the sacrifice of Isaac has baffled Jews and Christians alike, and the efforts to present the tale as something religiously palatable are endless and inventive. The easy way out is to claim that God was teasing: hardly an ennobling image of God, perhaps even impious. Another suggestion: Surprised by Abraham's obedience, God

Genesis 22

mercifully revoked the death sentence. Was Abraham being punished for loving only Isaac? For there was also his other son Ishmael. Soren Kierkegaard dragged Western philosophy into twentieth-century absurdity with his tortured probing of Abraham's ethical agony. Elie Wiesel identifies with Isaac, whose name means "Laughter" and who still could laugh after the holocaust. Historical critics wriggle out of the

Genesis 21:6

crisis of the text by seeing it as sociological commentary, the Hebrew repudiation of Canaanite infant sacrifice. But the story remains brutal.

Lesser sacrifices of all kinds—burnt offerings, peace offerings, sin offerings—fill the pages of the Hebrew Scriptures. Gideon sacrifices a goat and is rewarded by a vision of the blinding fire of God. Elijah proves to King Ahab and Queen Jezebel that the LORD is God when God descends on Mount Carmel in blazing fire to consume the bull on the altar. Hannah and Elkanah, a pious Hebrew couple, travel yearly to the shrine at Shiloh to present a thank offering to God; one year their offering is their weaned son Samuel, presented to the priest for a lifetime of service in the holy place. Much later, more direct meanings of religious sacrifice—gift to the gods, honor to the animals—were superseded, and the interior state of the worshiper became the true offering. Amos rants that God wants justice and righteousness, not sacrifice. So the tradition has assumed that dishonest intention was Cain's downfall.

The New Testament also is filled with sacrifice, this most primordial of religious ideas. Jesus' death was, after all, a secular execution, and numerous interpretations, or none at all, could be placed upon this event. From the earliest of Christian times the imagery of sacrifice was evoked. Paul writes that Christ "gave himself up for us, a fragrant offering and sacrifice to God," and he urges the faithful themselves to be "living sacrifices to God." The book of John compares Jesus to the Passover lamb and makes Jesus' crucifixion coincide with the slaughter of the lambs in the temple. The book of Hebrews elaborately develops the metaphor of Christ as the complete sacrifice. Even in the glorious vision of paradise, the Lamb is standing as though it had been slain.

We are not done with sacrifices in the church. Indeed, the idea of sacrifice has built the church, with the faithful called sometimes to sacrifice solely for the benefit of the institutional church. By the time of Anselm, Christian theology described Christ's crucifixion nearly exclu-

Judges 6:11–24

1 Kings 18:20–40

1 Samuel

Amos 5:21–24

Genesis 4:7

Ephesians 5:2

Romans 12:1

John 1:29
John 19:14

Hebrews 3—10

Revelation 5:6

sively in the language of sacrifice, and this sacrifice of Christ was to impel the sacrificial life of God's people. Of course, sacrifice meant one thing to a free Western male whose life's energy was focused on personal destiny, but meant quite another thing to an owned woman whose entire life, with or without God, was deprived of self-interest. Still today, however, lessons in which Christ urges self-denial are read repeatedly in the three-year lectionary, and we easily see as saints those who, like Dorothy Day, give up their lives for others.

Perhaps the greatest mystery is that this sacrifice of Isaac is no sacrifice at all. Is the tale a call to utter and complete sacrifice, as some preachers said in lenten sermons? Or is the story our reprieve from sacrifice, the ram in the thicket a paschal present to the faithful? Brother Eric, the iconographer at Taizé, has drawn Abraham and Isaac walking side by side, with a third bearded man walking behind, carrying the wood. Like an opal that you thought you knew but suddenly there is more and other fire in it, the story allures us, beckoning us to gaze into the fire, and where we thought there was only the terror of death, we see the hope of grace.

If creation can be seen as our birth story, the sacrifice of Isaac is our naming story. We bear our name in a world of moral ambiguity. Do we Christians heed Matthew's rigorous cry for moral perfection, exemplars of the Law? Or do we struggle along with Paul to live in love without the Law? Like Abraham, we are to trust, not in our own plans for the future, but in God. Like Abraham, we are saved from the horrors of religion, the incessant requirement to please an implacable God. Like Sarah, we are spared from sacrificing the fruit of our body for the sin of our soul. Like Isaac, we look up into the blade of death and see, instead, an angel. Like Christ, whose name we bear, we are given resurrection.

Matthew 5—7

Galatians 3—4

Micah 6:7

Christian iconography has used the story of the sacrifice of Isaac as a way to draw the crucifixion. Medieval holy books, frescoes and stained-glass windows presented parallel pictures of Isaac carrying the wood for the fire and Jesus carrying his cross, Abraham laying Isaac on the wood and Jesus being crucified. But on the night of the Paschal Vigil the story of the sacrifice of Isaac—which was not the sacrifice of Isaac—is far more a picture of the resurrection. Abraham walks before us holding high the burning flame, and we follow that light of Christ to the altar of our salvation. Abraham need not abandon his hope for progeny; Sarah need not grieve a dead son; Isaac need not face the sacrificial knife. Although death is right there, all around us, God will provide. We have traveled three days. On this mountain (Moriah? Golgotha?) we gather around the fire, and on this mountain life shall be provided.

AFTER THESE THINGS God tested Abraham, and said to him, "Abraham!" And he said, "Here am I." God said, "Take your son, your only son Isaac, whom you love, and go to the land of Moriah, and offer him there as a burnt offering upon one of the mountains of which I shall tell you." So Abraham rose early in the morning, saddled his donkey, and took two of his servants with him, and his son Isaac; and he cut the wood for the burnt offering, and arose and went to the place of which God had told him. On the third day Abraham lifted up his eyes and saw the place afar off. Then Abraham said to this servants, "Stay here with the donkey; I and the lad will go yonder and worship, and come again to you." And Abraham took the wood of the burnt offering, and laid it on Isaac his son; and he took in his hand the fire and the knife. So they went both of them together. And Isaac said to his father Abraham, "My father!" And he said, "Here am I, my son." Isaac said, "Behold, the fire and the wood; but where is the lamb for a burnt offering?" Abraham said, "God will provide the lamb for a burnt offering to God, my son." So they went both of them together.

When they came to the place of which God had told him, Abraham built an altar there, and laid the wood in order, and bound Isaac his son, and laid him on the altar, upon the wood. Then Abraham put forth his hand, and took the knife to slay his son. But the angel of the LORD called to him from heaven, and said, "Abraham, Abraham!" And he said, "Here am I." The angel said, "Do not lay your hand on the lad or do anything to him; for now I know that you fear God, seeing you have not withheld your son, your only son, from me." And Abraham lifted up his eyes and looked, and behold, behind him was a ram, caught in a thicket by its horns; and Abraham went and took the ram, and offered it up as a burnt offering instead of his son. So Abraham called the name of that place the LORD will provide; as it is said to this day, "On the mount of the LORD it shall be provided."

And the angel of the LORD called to Abraham a second time from heaven, and said, "By myself I have sworn, says the LORD, because you have done this, and have not withheld your son, your only son, I will indeed bless you, and I will multiply your descendants as the stars of heaven and as the sand which is on the seashore. And your descendants shall possess the gate of their enemies, and by your descendants shall all the nations of the earth bless themselves, because you have obeyed my voice."

We have heard our name,
O God of the twin mountain peaks.
We have followed the fire,
O God of the burning stars.
Lead us to sacrifice;
save us from sacrifice;
and may we laugh in your presence,
through Christ the living one.

THE SCRIPTURES depict the human predicament in different ways. Abraham and Sarah are childless in old age, but they want their line to live. God meets their need with an heir. The widow of Zarephath is starving. God feeds her miraculously with a larder that never empties. Naaman has a physical problem, leprosy. He and many others in the scriptures seek health, and God cures them. Job's quest, on the other hand, is philosophical: What is the relationship between God and human suffering? Job does not receive intellectual satisfaction, but a vision of God. The human predicament as depicted in the Bible that has become most central to Western Christian consciousness is sin. We may or may not be dying of hunger or afflicted with disease; nevertheless, like Adam and Eve, like Cain, like David, we have sinned, and what we seek from God is forgiveness.

Genesis 15:1–6

1 Kings 17:8–16

2 Kings 5

Job 3, 40

The Christianity that nurtured me was intensely aware of sin, high on obedience to law and low on rebellion against authority. The order of government was seen as an arm of God, sometimes to embrace us, sometimes to throttle us, and we were to knuckle under. After all,

Exodus 14–15

said my parochial school teachers, Jesus did not counsel the disciples toward revolution against the Roman Empire. He befriended those in collusion with the enemy; he said his kingdom was not of this world. Paul even sends a runaway slave back to servitude.

Matthew 26:52

John 18:36

Philemon 8–13

Christianity, however, did not originate as a benediction of the structures of society. At its beginnings the church was a countercultural community of believers. Only in the fourth century, after the peace of

Constantine, did the church become an official religion of the Holy Roman Empire. Since then, too easily and too often middle- and upper-class Christians, comfortable within the social order, have ignored the human predicament of oppression.

Here on Easter Eve is the preeminent narrative of God's Hebrew people: their deliverance from oppression. God saves the people not merely from individual pain or psychological distress: God saves the whole people from a life too close to death. No more will the males be worked to death or murdered as infants, leaving the women to be maids and mistresses. In this deliverance an entire people receives its identity and its mission, reclaiming its freedom as humankind before God. In the crossing of the Red Sea are signs of God's power aplenty: Moses' *Exodus 14:21–29* hand, the angel of God, the pillar of fire, the east wind, the safe shore. The people know the power of God not because they were taught to believe it but because that power freed them from oppression.

The story is an archetypal, masculine hero story on the grandest scale. A man is determined to lead his people to freedom. He opposes the evil powers and in a contest of divine feats proves his superior might. In the last great battle, with the enemy army upon him, he is able to lead the masses across the sea to a new land. There the journey continues: up the mountain of God, across the wilderness, to yet another shore, the Jordan, water again becoming the barrier and the path to new life. Yet this hero story focuses not on Moses but on the God who called Moses, effected the miracles, sent the plagues, led the people, camouflaged their camp, parted the sea and destroyed the enemy. It is to God, not to Moses, that the women dance and sing.

This story has a feminine counterpart in the narrative of Hagar. Hagar has been a household slave, both maid to the lady and mistress *Genesis 16* to the lord. She was thrown out of the house, which was never her home, to survive or die in the wilderness with her son. She finds a well and mothers her son back to strength; they thrive as a new race upon the earth. This heroine story also focuses on God: God is the one who provides the mysterious well so that Hagar and Ishmael live. Like Moses and his throngs, Hagar and her child are runaway slaves saved by God through water.

The tale of the rescue from Egypt is also a woman's story. Biblical scholars are intrigued by the two parts of Exodus 15: In the first part Moses leads the people in a long psalm of praise, and in the second part Miriam with her timbrel leads the women in a victory dance. Many scholars hypothesize that the older story was that of Miriam the prophet leading the women in song and dance. The chant assigned to her appears more primitive than the complex poem associated with Moses. These scholars speculate that in the centuries of storytelling and in the transcription of the oral stories to written texts, the prominence of Miriam gave way to the authority of Moses. Such scholars cite the passage in the prophet Micah in which God names Moses, Aaron and Miriam as the trio who lead the people from bondage. *Micah 6:4*

Exodus 15:1–18
Exodus 15:20–21

Perhaps those revising the lectionary could expand this vigil lesson to include Exodus 15:20–21 rather than Exodus 15:1. We should not miss the opportunity to recall the deeds of Miriam, who led her people in rejoicing for the salvation by God. The Hebrew name Miriam is the Greek name Mary; all those New Testament women are named after their great matriarch who led the song of victory.

Mary's Magnificat is an apt reflection on this narrative of the rescue from Egypt, for Mary, too, rejoices that God reverses the world order. Monarchs are deposed; the rich go away hungry. In the terms of the Israelites' narrative, slaves are freed, a cavalry is foiled, even the laws of the created universe are reversed to make a path for the mercy of God. Miriam rejoices that the horse and its rider have been thrown *Luke 1:46–55* into the sea, and by her chant, as by Mary's Magnificat, all our security in society's status quo is challenged.

Millennia of the oppression of peoples and groups have not taught us to live in justice. If anything, humankind has only perfected the means of oppression. The liberation theologians of this century plead that the whole church, like the God of Exodus, hears the cries of the suffering people, that we like Moses lead the people to freedom and like Miriam dance at the demise of oppressors. During the 1960s an antiwar song challenged Americans' self-appointed sense of manifest destiny: The stanzas told a one-sided version of the history of our wars, and the refrain repeated that the wars were all justified because we had "God on our side." Miriam's ecstasy is disarming: Are we Israel or are we Egypt in the ancient narrative?

The church too easily responds, "Oh, we are Israel, for the sea is baptism." That the sea is indeed baptism makes this facile answer unfaithful, for our baptism calls us to lead others out of bondage. Baptism does not anoint the status quo. In baptism we get washed ashore one with all the other drowning folk. No longer can the "haves" be content: What we "have" after crossing the baptismal sea is a flood of refugees, of the unemployed, of the disenfranchised, of those who are despised and rejected. The narrative of the deliverance from Egypt gives Easter a metaphor for Christ's resurrection: The Spirit of God is turning human life upside down.

THE LORD said to Moses, "Why do you cry to me? Tell the people of Israel to go forward. Lift up your rod, and stretch out your hand over the sea and divide it, that the people of Israel may go on dry ground through the sea. And I will harden the hearts of the Egyptians so that they shall go in after them, and I will get glory over Pharoah and all his host, his chariots, and his horsemen. And the Egyptians shall know that I am the LORD, when I have gotten glory over the Pharaoh, his chariots, and his horsemen."

Then the angel of God who went before the host of Israel moved and went behind them; and the pillar of cloud moved from before them and stood behind them, coming between the host of Egypt and the host of Israel. And there was the cloud and the darkness; and the night passed without one coming near the other all night.

Then Moses stretched out his hand over the sea; and the LORD drove the sea back by a strong east wind all night, and made the sea dry land, and the waters were divided. And the people of Israel went into the midst of the sea on dry ground, the waters being a wall to them on their right hand and on the left. The Egyptians pursued, and went in after them into the midst of the sea, all the Pharoah's horses, his chariots, and his horsemen. And in the morning watch the LORD in the pillar of fire and of cloud looked down upon the host of the Egyptians, and discomfited the host of the Egyptians, clogging their chariot wheels so that they drove heavily; and the Egyptians said, "Let us flee from before Israel; for the LORD fights for them against the Egyptians."

Then the LORD said to Moses, "Stretch out your hand over the sea, that the water may come back upon the Egyptians, upon their chariots, and upon their horsemen." So Moses stretched forth his hand over the sea, and the sea returned to its wonted flow when the morning appeared; and the Egyptians fled into it, and the LORD routed the Egyptians in the midst of the sea. The waters returned and covered the chariots and the horsemen and all the host of Pharoah that had followed them into the sea; not so much as one of them remained. But the people of Israel walked on dry ground through the sea, the waters being a wall to them on their right hand and on their left.

Thus the LORD saved Israel that day from the hand of the Egyptians; and Israel saw the Egyptians dead upon the seashore. And Israel saw the great work which the LORD did against the Egyptians, and the people feared the LORD; and they believed in the LORD and in Moses, the servant of the LORD.

Then Moses and the people of Israel sang this song to the LORD, saying, "I will sing to the LORD who has triumphed gloriously; the horse and its rider have been thrown into the sea."

O merciful God,
save all whom oppression drowns.
Wash away injustice.
With Miriam
we sing to the majestic mercy
of your baptismal waters.
O merciful God,
we implore you: This time
save also the Egyptians
in your mercy wider and deeper
than all the oceans of the earth.

WHAT IS REDEMPTION LIKE? How can we picture the baptized life? With the catechumens asking questions such as these, we read three stanzas from the poem in Isaiah 54. Each stanza develops an image of salvation, and the poem ties the three images together with key words. The reading is a primer in biblical imagery, both in its presentation of three central metaphors for salvation and in its freedom to use ancient images, to interweave one simile with another, to rely on the richness of poetry in describing the mercy of God. The prophet proclaims the good news that we are embraced by God's arms, we are safe in the ark, we are secure in the city, despite evidence to the contrary.

The first stanza likens salvation to marriage with God. It is a common ancient idea that the universe was created by a cosmic mar- *Isaiah 54:5–8* riage in which Father Sky embraced Mother Earth to give birth to the world. In attempting to understand life and to control their universe, human beings projected their own sexuality into the sky: Deity was divided by gender distinctions into gods and goddesses, tales of the

Isaiah 54

sexual exploits of the deities filled religious imagination, and ritualized sexual relations had sacral significance in the community. Primitive figurines with greatly exaggerated sexual organs, now displayed in archaeological museums, demonstrate the ancient link between religious power and human sexuality. This primitive myth, told in various guises throughout the world, became central to the legends and rituals of the Canaanite religion and was thus an ever-present backdrop to the religious beliefs and practices of the Hebrew tribes.

Israel resisted this impressive package with admirable conviction: God has no gender and was not a primal father or mother of the human race. Divinity was a power different from and beyond human sexuality. To create, God did not mate but spoke. Biblical traditions teach no tales or rituals in which human sexuality reenacts maleness or femaleness in God, and later Hebrew theologians inveigh against the entire symbolic system of deified gender. Perhaps behind the proscription against "graven images" was well-placed fear that, with humankind perpetually obsessed with sex, the bull and the pole too easily would find their way back into religious practice.

But Israel's caution with sexual metaphors did not mean that the marriage image was wholly rejected. For Israel, the truth of the image is not about God's sexuality but about God's love. Hebrew poetry uses the marriage metaphor to depict God's union not with nature or with another deity but with the chosen people. Hebrew poems liken God to Israel's husband and Israel to God's wife. God has loved us and married us. In case the image made the hearer think of Baal, the Canaanite husband-god, the stanza reminds us that we are wed to no archetypal bull, but to our Maker, the Holy One of Israel, our Redeemer, the God of the whole earth. The human image is being asked to describe the transcendent God. The poet borrows the Canaanite imagery but hastens to proclaim the LORD and to clarify the truth of the metaphor. To be married to God is not to quake before a powerful lord—the name Baal means master—but to rejoice in God's loving arms.

Yet the poem is no mushy wedding ditty. The poet cites the evidence that there has been a divorce. God admits that there was a temporary separation. But the people still feel abandoned. Their situation is dreadful, and they are more ready to believe in God's wrath than in God's compassion. The people feel cast off by God's arm, rather than embraced. The prophet calls the people back to life with God.

God has married them and is bound to them in covenant even when they experience rejection and imagine punishment.

We contemporary Christians can use this ancient metaphor responsibly only after we acknowledge its misuse in our past. Hefty scholarly studies now trace the combined power of Platonic idealism, religious celibacy, the cultural status of women and single-sex hierarchy to distort the truth of the marriage image. Even scientific ignorance played its part in this—centuries of the faithful erroneously considered the entire infant to be in the sperm, the woman providing nothing but a passive womb. This helped propel the metaphor of cosmic marriage to inappropriate ends. The Hebrew proscription against graven images was wise, for the metaphor too easily gets carved in stone; medieval Christians were stimulated by this metaphor and used it to make claims about the gender of God, the nature of the church and sexual roles in ways that now seem narrowly time-bound and unjustly sexist.

"O, my luve is like a red red rose," wrote the Scottish poet Robert Burns. In some ways yes and in other ways no! So although the marriage metaphor cannot say all that medieval Christianity foisted upon it, the image can uniquely express some truths about God's covenant of love. For divorce statistics notwithstanding, there is still in Western imagination the myth of the perfect marriage, the bond that lasts all of life and beyond death, deepening companionship, faithful interdependence, maturing ecstasy. In Isaiah the man embraces the woman. In the Song of Songs, the woman actively searches for her lover and calls *Song of Songs 3:1–3* him to her bed. The Hebrew poems go richly in both ways, God the husband, God the wife, God the lover, God the beloved.

Lest we become too enamored of the marriage metaphor, Isaiah 54 sets it aside for the image of Noah's flood. Here again is memory of *Isaiah 54:9–10* an ancient human story, that a great flood covered the world and that some few with their animals survived in a boat. The Hebrew Scriptures *Genesis 7—9* tell this story in wondrous detail. As in the story of Moses, God receives the praise: God condemns the filth of the world, God washes its evil away, God saves the faithful, God ensures a renewed universe, God promises an everlasting covenant of peace. Noah's flood is an early resurrection story: God is re-creating the world. Yet again the poet acknowledges evidence to the contrary. We do not feel secure. We see the mountains moving around; the very universe is threatened. Despite this, the poem woos us to trust in the ark God sends.

Already in the First Letter of Peter the story of Noah's ark is *1 Peter 3:18–22* brought into the imagery of the church. Christians recall this story when they call their church's building a nave, the word nave derived from the Latin *navis,* boat, as we sail together in this ark across baptismal waters into peace with God. But the New Testament urges against a simple allegorical interpretation of the story. It is not that the flood waters wash the dirt from us or that our little churchy structure is the whole ark and everyone else is drowning, drowning. Rather, baptism, like the ark, saves us through the resurrection of Jesus Christ from the dead. The words that occurred in the marriage stanza—compassion and love—recur here. God's ark, like the raising of Jesus from the dead, is a sign of divine compassion and love.

In the beginning of the third stanza, the prophet acknowledges *Isaiah 54:11–14* that we are storm-tossed. Floods are raging, both the flood of the world's destruction and the flood of baptismal might. We, more conscious of being tossed by the storm than of being saved in the ark, are brought finally to the safety of the city. Although the Hebrew tribes originally were nomads, once settled in Canaan they began to use the *Psalms 84* image of the city as a symbol of peace and security. In Hebrew imagery *Jonah 2* the sea is the dreaded place of chaos, the home of the monster. Thus at the end of time, says Revelation, the sea will be no more, and the city *Revelation 21:1* will be the home of all the wandering peoples. Christian imagery is not reactionary, finding only in the distant past its images for life. Our scriptures begin in a garden but end in the city.

We now are coming into the city, with the assembly of all the faithful. Life in communion with others promises to be safe and beautiful. No ordinary city, this culmination of human life is made of magnificent jewels. Its foundations are constructed of sapphire, and its battlements glisten not with warriors' shields, but with rubies. We know this image best from its lavish description in Revelation, which the church reads during the 50 days of Easter. In the resurrection we are brought into this city, where there is wisdom and prosperity, righteousness and peace for us and our children. In this city we live secure, protected by walls of radiant beauty created by the power of God.

Revelation 21:18–21

That's a lot in one reading. Marriage to a beloved God, safety in the storm-tossed ark, security in the bejeweled city, all in ten verses whip on by, too quick a reminder of three of the richest metaphors in the Christian tradition. God's arms become the sides of the ship become the crystal walls. Lover is ark is home.

THUS SAYS THE LORD:

For your Maker is as your husband,
   whose name is the LORD of hosts;
and the Holy One of Israel is your Redeemer,
   who is called the God the whole earth.
For the LORD has called you
   as a wife forsaken and grieved in spirit,
as a wife of youth when she is cast off,
   says your God.
For a brief moment I forsook you,
   but with great compassion I will gather you.
In overflowing wrath for a moment
   I hid my face from you,
but with everlasting love I will have compassion on you,
   says the LORD, your Redeemer.

For this is like the days of Noah to me:
   as I swore that the waters of Noah
   should no more go over the earth,
so I have sworn that I will not be angry with you
   and will not rebuke you.
For the mountains may depart
   and the hills be removed,
but my steadfast love shall not depart from you,
   and my covenant of peace shall not be removed,
   says the LORD, who has compassion on you.

O afflicted one, storm-tossed, and not comforted,
 behold, I will set your stones in antimony,
 and lay your foundations with sapphires.
I will make your pinnacles of agate,
 your gates of carbuncles,
 and all your wall of precious stones.
All your children shall be taught by the LORD,
 and great shall be the prosperity of your offspring.
In righteousness you shall be established;
 you shall be far from oppression, for you shall not fear;
 and from terror, for it shall not come near you.

O God,
mad lover,
faithful beloved,
sturdy ark,
perpetual rainbow,
jeweled city,
peaceful home,
you are our salvation.
We rise to life in you
through Christ the living one.

HO! COME TO THE FEAST! Here finally is a banquet without cost, the gift of endless food for countless throngs. The hungry have come from the east and the west, from the ancient past and from this morning, to dine at God's magnificent meal. So who all is here?

At the head of the table are Adam and Eve, feasting contentedly on all the fruits of the garden, save one. There is Abraham alongside three visitors dining on cakes, a calf and curds, the same menu they shared when the three announced to him and Sarah the birth of a son. All the people of Israel are crowding around the table, murmuring over their manna, gratified with the quail, enlivened by the water that poured from the rock and awaiting the milk and honey. Here the spies come up to the table, bearing between them the produce pillaged from the promised land: the mammoth bunch of grapes, the pomegranates and the figs. Further down the table of God is Ruth and her mother-in-law Naomi, who have journeyed from the famine in Moab and in their search for barley have come here to Bethlehem, which means the House of Bread.

Genesis 2:9

Genesis 18:1–9

Exodus 16:1–21

Exodus 3:8

Ruth 1:6

Numbers 13:23

Isaiah 55

Many of the pious are surprised to see that the fugitive David has arrived, sweating from his escape from King Saul and nearly starving; he is wolfing down the holy bread from the tabernacle, which seems to be the only food that God laid within his grasp. That woman there is the widow of Zarephath, whose name has been forgotten, but whose larder we remember as being forever full of oil and meal. For dinner music a singer chants from the scroll of Isaiah: "On this mountain the

1 Samuel 21:1–6

1 Kings 17:8–16

LORD of hosts will make for all peoples a feast of fat things."

For the table, thousands of years long, now is also the crowded

slopes of the mountain on which Jesus orders the people to be seated in groups of hundreds and fifties. What seems to be only a child's lunch

satisfies 5,000 men, "besides women and children," Matthew adds (aware that at this new table setting not only the men are counted). There is the daughter of Jairus, newly raised from death, whose parents

were told by Jesus to give her something to eat.

There we see the two disciples dining simply on a Sunday supper

at Emmaus, when suddenly they recognize the risen Lord is at table with them. And there are the disciples describing this feast as a fish

breakfast by the sea: For, as the gospel of John has it, the miraculous catch of fish is not an impressive object lesson to lure the fishermen to

the task of preaching, but rather a sign after the resurrection that the feast of God invites even the apostate Peter to eat all he can. As John Chrysostom preached at a Paschal Vigil about 1,600 years ago, "Let all the pious and all lovers of God rejoice in the splendor of this feast. . . . Those who have toiled since the first hour, let them now receive their due reward; let any who came after the third hour be grateful to join in the feast, and those who may have come after the sixth, let them not be afraid of being too late. . . . You the first and you the last, receive alike your reward." Ho! Come to the feast!

Isaiah 55 says that the promise of this feast is the same promise made to King David: God will steadfastly love the chosen people. Israel had come to hope that it would be blessed through the king. Having a king at all was Israel's cultural adaptation to its Canaanite neighbors, for even today monarchies look attractive to peoples without

them. King David became a sign of God's covenant with the people— just as God dispensed power through the divine regent, so God would shower love down to the royal people. It was as if God's covenant were

mediated through the monarchy. Although Israel soon discovered that
a throne does not ensure justice—one of Solomon's innovations was to
turn subject peoples into slaves—the image of an ideal monarch pervades Hebrew poetry. There will be a day, the poets dream, in which a
perfect sovereign will govern in beneficence and whose power will
effect justice in the land. The deeds of such a monarch would guaran-
tee salvation for all the people, for through the king God would save.

1 Kings 9:15–21

Isaiah 9:2–7

And so when the Israelites were again dispossessed and became
exiles under foreign domination, when their own monarchy had been
crushed, they told the story of Queen Esther. With beauty and cunning
and courage, Esther overcomes Haman and his forces of evil and saves
her people from genocide. Ho! Come to the feast! Queen Esther, like
the monarchs we hoped for of old, has saved her people from destruction, and we come to the table of the LORD for feasting and gladness.

Esther 8:3–6

Still today Orthodox Jews give away food to strangers on the festival of Purim to celebrate the victory of so great a queen. Part of the
Purim menu is a cookie called Hamantaschen, "Haman's purses." These
small three-cornered tarts are named after the dread enemy, for at this
table we need no longer fear our foes. In fact, we eat them up. So the
rabbis imagined that the main course of the feast at the end of time
will be the Leviathan, the dreaded sea monster cut up and served as
banquet of life for the faithful.

Ho! Come to the feast! We come, wanting to eat supper with
Jesus, like the disciples did, fretting because the Last Supper was so very
long ago. John's gospel shows us how to feast with Jesus. It does not
even narrate the menu, but instead says of Christ, "I am the bread of
life." So Christ is the feast, and on this single Life Tree is variety
indeed, the twelve fruits that fill us to the full growing on one single
tree. Ho! Here are pomegranates for Adam and Eve, elderberries for
Abraham and Sarah, lemons for Moses and Miriam, dates for Ruth
and Boaz, olives for the widow and Elijah, grapes for the disciples and

John 6:35

Revelation 22:2

the uncounted women, sugarplums for Jairus and his daughter, passion fruit for King David, Persian melons for Queen Esther, hagberries for John Chrysostom, plus your favorite for you and my favorite for me, all on one tree planted by our God. Ho! It is all here, both milk and monster meat, in the bread and wine, all on one table served by our God. For the bread and wine, like Abraham's curds and the widow's meal, are but the first course of that final banquet that will be not only bread and wine but feast for all forever. We will dine on the very life of God.

HO, EVERY ONE who thirsts,
 come to the waters;
and whoever has no money,
 come, buy and eat!
Come, buy wine and milk
 without money and without price.
Why do you spend your money for that which is not bread,
 and your labor for that which does not satisfy?
Hearken diligently to me, and eat what is good,
 and delight yourselves in fatness.
Incline your ear, and come to me;
 hear, that your soul may live;
and I will make with you an everlasting covenant,
 my steadfast, sure love for David.
Behold, I made him a witness to the peoples,
 a leader and commander for the peoples.
Behold, you shall call nations that you know not,
 and nations that knew you not shall run to you,
because of the LORD your God, and of the Holy One of Israel,
 for the LORD has glorified you.
Seek the LORD while the LORD may be found,
 call upon God, while God is near;
let the wicked forsake their ways,
 and the unrighteous their thoughts;
let them return to the LORD, who will have mercy on them,
 and to our God, who will abundantly pardon.

For my thoughts are not your thoughts,
    neither are your ways my ways, says the LORD.
For as the heavens are higher than the earth,
    so are my ways higher than your ways
    and my thoughts than your thoughts.
For as the rain and the snow come down from heaven,
    and return not thither but water the earth,
making it bring forth and sprout,
    giving seed to the sower and bread to the eater,
so shall my word be that goes forth from my mouth;
    it shall not return to me empty,
but it shall accomplish that which I purpose,
    and prosper in the thing for which I sent it.

Blessed are you,
O Lord our God,
who brings forth bread from the earth.
Blessed are you,
bread for the world,
wine for the wedding,
fruits on the tree,
milk and honey for the journey,
lamb for the end of time.
Blessed be God.
Amen.

THE HEBREW WORD FOR WISDOM is *hokmah,* and from the earliest times the Hebrew tribes valued it highly. When the people were nomads, they cultivated folk traditions of advice that sought health and happiness for the people. Perhaps the proscription against pork originated in primitive folk wisdom concerning the danger of trichinosis. When the Hebrew tribes became a kingdom, they imported from Egypt a monarchical tradition of court advisers and then began collecting writings urging those around the king to standards of behavior and to advancement in learning. During the exile the wisdom movement matured into a rich literary treasury. The existential question of the exiled people—what does it mean to be a Jew?—spurred on the creativity of the learned who recorded their wisdom through sages such as Baruch and articulated their doubts in characters such as Job. Increasing contact with the Greek philosophical tradition in the several centuries before Christ added to these collections poetically cast theories of how wisdom is acquired and what areas of learning it includes.

Baruch 3—4

Although the primitive aphorisms claimed that in all creation humankind alone can be wise, later sages ascribed wisdom to God alone, who chose to bestow it on the chosen people.

An imaginative part of this wisdom literature is the body of Lady Wisdom poems. The books of Proverbs, Wisdom, Sirach and Baruch each contain chapter-length poems in which wisdom is personified as a great lady, a goddess figure who symbolizes wisdom and invites the people to participate in her life. Perhaps merely the grammatical fact that *hokmah* was a noun of feminine gender led the poets into this linguistic trick. For the later Jewish poets writing in Greek, the noun was again feminine, *sophia*. Perhaps the perennial urge to honor a mother goddess led the poets to see in Lady Wisdom at least a metaphoric goddess. Perhaps the tradition of wise women in the ancient nomad culture developed into this feminized tribute to human knowledge and insight.

Lady Wisdom is depicted as standing at her door or crying through the marketplace, beckoning to the wayward to follow her steps to learning. She warns the people of impending disaster if they follow instead Dame Folly, the foolish wanton woman who is never far off. "I will make my words known to you," she promises in the introduction to the Proverbs, and in the way of wisdom the people will live securely. "My mouth will utter truth," she claims. The ways of knowledge are better than jewels, silver and gold. A recurring idea in these poems is that in creating the world, God first created Lady Wisdom, and as God's companion and delight she cooperated in laying out the universe. Now she serves bread and wine at her table, summons all to enter her house and to be filled with the fruits of wisdom.

The Book of Wisdom calls her radiant and urges everyone who wants to succeed to follow her light. She is more beautiful than the sun, an emanation of the glorious God. The book retells the narratives of the Hebrew people, crediting Lady Wisdom with knowledge and righteousness, loyalty and power. A long poem said to be words of Solomon tells of his choosing her above all else.

In the Book of Sirach, Lady Wisdom herself is praised for creating the universe and for coming to dwell on earth in the people of Israel. The fruits on her table satisfy all the world. Lady Wisdom is queen of the universe, with her throne on the pillar of cloud that was to the people of Israel the sign of God's presence. Lady Wisdom then is described as the tree of life, greater than all the famous trees of the

Proverbs 1:23

Proverbs 8:22–23

Proverbs 9:2

Wisdom 7:7–10

Wisdom 7—9

Sirach 24:1–8

Sirach 24:9–12

Sirach 24:13–17

ancient Near East. The old image of the fruits on her table become in this poem the fruits on the branches of her as world tree.

In the poem from Baruch read at the Vigil, the catechumens, and we with them, are searching for Lady Wisdom. We have come a long way looking for life and peace and understanding: Where is wisdom? We cannot find her anywhere on this earth—part of the poem omitted from the reading lists all the cities and countries where seekers have failed to discover her. Ah! But God, the creator of the universe, found her and gave her to Israel. She is "the book of the commandments of God," the words that bring life to God's people. Lady Wisdom resides in these Hebrew Scriptures.

Baruch 3:15

Baruch 3:22–23

Baruch 4:1

Of course wisdom is no more a great lady in the sky than God is a great man in the sky. But these poets, praising in a tongue that rendered God as masculine, balanced out the gender of their religious longing by locating in Lady Wisdom much that belongs to divinity. She is teacher of truth, creator of the universe, giver of food, light of all, the power behind kings, tree of life. She is the sacred writings, the word of God. For the church, the longing for Lady Wisdom is realized in Christ. Strangely, this weak man is our wisdom, writes Paul to the Corinthians. Christ is teacher, creator, light, the personification of the word of God around which we gather to receive life. In subsequent theological speculation, the feminine noun *sophia*, wisdom, gave way to the masculine noun *logos*, word, and thus honor to Lady Wisdom gets lost to the church, replaced by the praise of the Word in John's gospel. Yet when the fourteenth-century English mystic Julian lauded the Trinity, she called the second person "God All-wisdom, our natural mother," as again the wisdom of God was imaged as a feminine trait.

1 Corinthians 1:21

John 1:1–18

Feminine trait, masculine trait, who can say? Although we know that every culture trains boys and girls to act out different values, we have yet to discover whether any personality predispositions come tied to gender. I know wise men; I know wise women. But it is illuminating that in a culture in which communal leadership and social power were increasingly monopolized by men, wisdom was granted to a woman, to one outside the power structure. Even the grandeur of Solomon defers to the magnificence of Lady Wisdom. Perhaps the tradition of these poems attests to a contemporary truth known also among the ancients that the wisdom of God is not found in the power brokers of the society. The very poets and scribes who perpetuated the wisdom movement praised God for Lady Wisdom and depicted the truth of God's word as a cosmic hostess, teacher and guide.

Eastern iconography and later Romanesque sculpture came to depict the Virgin Mother in regal and stately formality as if she were herself a chair, with the young Christ child on her lap blessing the people. This image was called "the throne of wisdom," the cosmic queen Lady Wisdom become Mary, who is also the throne bearing the child Wisdom. So the magi, traveling from the East to find a king, come to *Matthew 2:11* kneel before a child on a mother's lap. The image is rich: Lady Wisdom is Christ, Lady Wisdom is Mary, Lady Wisdom is God herself. From this wisdom comes truth, and we walk her path this Easter to life.

HEAR THE COMMANDMENTS of life, O Israel;
    give ear, and learn wisdom!
Why is it, O Israel, why is it that you are in the land of your enemies,
    that you are growing old in a foreign country,
that you are defiled with the dead,
    that you are counted among those in Hades?
You have forsaken the fountain of wisdom.
If you had walked in the way of God,
    you would be dwelling in peace for ever.
Learn where there is wisdom,
    where there is strength,
    where there is understanding,
that you may at the same time discern
    where there is length of days, and life,
    where there is light for the eyes, and peace.
Who has found the place of Wisdom?
    And who has entered her storehouses?
The one who knows all things knows her,
    and found her through understanding.
The one who prepared the earth for all time
    filled it with four-footed creatures;
the one who sends forth the light, and it goes,
    called it, and it hearkened in fear;
the stars shone in their watches, and were glad;
    God called them, and they said, "Here we are!"
    They shone with gladness for the one who made them.

This is our God,
    with whom none other can be compared.
God found the whole way to knowledge,
    and gave her to Jacob, God's servant,
    and to Israel, the one whom God loved.
Afterward she appeared upon earth
    and lived among humankind.
She is the book of the commandments of God,
    and the law that endures for ever.
All who hold her fast will live,
    and those who forsake her will die.
Turn, O Jacob, and take her;
    walk toward the shining of her light.
Do not give your glory to another,
    or your advantages to an alien people.
Happy are we, O Israel,
    for we know what is pleasing to God.

O Lady Wisdom,
we laud your light,
we follow your path,
we feast at your table.
By your words,
which are meat and drink indeed,
give us the wisdom
that comes only from you.

THE BIBLE CONTAINS many patterns of images. The Vigil readings have immersed us in some of them: God as fire, creation as gift, sacrifice as religion, food as grace, to name a few. A common complaint heard these days is that the images of the Bible are archaic, lost in the past, dead bones to offer a hungry world. But the last Vigil lesson addresses a theme that pervades both the scriptures and today's news: the quest for a homeland.

Our city streets today house an increasing number of homeless people. Some, but only a few, have a history of mental illness, having been released from institutions without the necessary supports available. Some are employed at minimum-skill jobs, and the minimum wage cannot pay both food and housing. Some are unemployed: high-school graduates who cannot read well enough to fill out job applications, middle-aged veterans trained only in guerrilla warfare, old homemakers who never have worked in the marketplace. Some were self-sufficient middle-class folk, but a series of disasters—ill health, a house fire, job loss, several deaths at once—have knocked them over

Ezekiel 36

the edge. Some have taken to the streets to escape violence at home. More than half have no history of drug or alcohol abuse. More than one-fourth are children under 16.

We gather in such a world to read the scriptures, and we discover homelessness a recurrent theme of God's people. Read consecutively book by book, the Bible can be seen as a history of people seeking a homeland. For whatever reason, far back in prehistory, the Semitic nomads came to ache for a homeland, a place of settled peace and

Genesis 12:4–9 communal wholeness. Genesis says that Abram and Sarai journeyed to
such a promised land and thus began the story of the Israelites. Isaac
inherited Abraham's promise and passed the blessing to Jacob, the

Genesis 27:5–29 younger son who, helped by his mother, tricked his elder brother Esau
out of the prized legacy. The 12 family tribes then immigrated to Egypt

Genesis 46:1–7 to survive the famine, and the book of Exodus finds them, once
nomads, now slaves, homeless still. Moses was called to lead the tribes

Exodus 3:7–9 back to the promised land, but the path was arduous and indirect. No
longer slaves, they now were wanderers, refugees, homeless still. Finally

Joshua 3:14–17 in the book of Joshua the people cross the Jordan River into Canaan to
claim the gift of the land.

Although Israel now resided on the land, the hope for a homeland was not satisfied. The books of Joshua and Judges tell of "the
conquest," for the Canaanite inhabitants were a formidable obstacle to
be absorbed, moved around, driven out, slaughtered, so that the land
was free to occupy. And when the land was more or less Israel's, the
deep desire for *shalom* still was not realized; as the histories of Samuel
and Kings narrate, the desire for a perfect home was expressed in the
yearning for a monarchy. If only our land were a kingdom, say the
tribal leaders, it would be truly a homeland! Thus began the saga of the
kings of Israel and Judah: Saul, David, Solomon, followed by lesser and
weaker men who finally conceded their failure when the kingdom was
destroyed. Over the royal din of warfare, political machinations and
idolatry, what we call "the major prophets" record the dream of a
homeland that would ensure justice, not might, and loyalty to God and
neighbor, not selfish opportunism.

In the sixth century before Christ the monarchy was dissolved,
the landed people homeless once again, living as aliens among the vic-
tors. While they cried out their lamentations, the dream revived: Ah,

that God might bring us back to the land! When under Ezra they finally returned to their homeland, the occupying armies remained. Thus the longing was still not abated: Ah, for our own dominion, cry more prophetic voices! So it was that in John's gospel, when Jesus provided bread in the wilderness, the crowd wished to set him up as king. *John 6:15* "The King of the Jews" read his sentencing, and in the book of Acts, *John 19:19* the disciples who gathered on the Mount of Olives on the 40th day after the resurrection still are expressing this very same hope: "Lord, will you at this time restore dominion to Israel?" The New Testament *Acts 1:6* concludes with a variant of the homeland image, as homeland-become-monarchy-become-city descends from heaven, and the home of God becomes the home for the people. *Revelation 21:2–3*

The Europeans who settled North America sought a homeland no less than had the Hebrew people. The Protestants, traversing the sea for religious rights, were inspired by their faith in God's gift of a homeland. Like the Israelites, they assumed they had God on their side. They absorbed, moved about, drove out and slaughtered the native peoples, in order to free up the land for themselves. The early novelist James Fenimore Cooper praised the idyllic settling of this new homeland; the poet Walt Whitman sang ecstatically of the new land of America. What came to be called manifest destiny is merely a secularized version of the conviction that God intended this people to have a homeland, a place of personal peace and communal security.

Even in the twentieth century, authors from the United States use a location, whether a New England town or a Mississippi county, as a microcosm of the homeland. Home is described now both as palace and prison. In the drama of this century, one play after another— *Desire Under the Elms, The Glass Menagerie, Death of a Salesman, Raisin in the Sun*—has squeezed the dream for a homeland onto the stage by focusing the action of the play in a family's house. In each of these plays the struggle for human meaning is expressed in a conflict over who lives in the house, who pays for the house, who inherits the house, who escapes from the house. Here the ancient hope for a homeland is located in the American scramble for an estate in the suburbs with a patio and a pool. Yet several blocks from affluent streets are again the homeless, searching through the ages for a land.

The fortunate know the dream of the homeland by living out its realization. Teenagers staple posters on the ceiling of their rooms, a single woman finally fulfills a personal fantasy of carpeting her home in powder blue, a couple vacations another year in a cabin by the lake, a family returns to the United States after too long a journey abroad, an old man enters a retirement home that boasts all the amenities a life's savings can buy. The fortunate reside in their contentment as a homeland itself; for these few the frantic pilgrimage is laid aside for a time.

But many people still make their life's decisions in a search for a perfect home. Attempts in the 1960s at "churches without walls," worshiping assemblies who rented existing facilities in order to escape the bondage of land ownership, have failed, as members sought the security of a nearby parish with its handy parking lot. The conversion of apartment houses into condominiums is not merely a means of tax relief in a capitalist economy: It also signals the human longing of owning one's own home. The dream merrily expands: The upper middle class, feeling imprisoned in their homes that are hardly peaceful havens, is strapped for cash because of mortgage payments on lakefront property. I know also that a celibate diocesan priest must ache for a home; I do not know how he comes to satisfy this primordial need. And if we are lucky, all these folk bring these archetypal longings with them to the annual Paschal Vigil.

The Easter Vigil's reading of Ezekiel promises us the resurrection in the terms of this archetypal longing. The first half of the book of Ezekiel condemns the people for their misuse of the land, their lawless-

Ezekiel 1—24

62

ness, injustice and apostasy. But after the exile from the land in 587 BCE, the prophet proclaims once again the promise of a homeland: God will reconstitute the people Israel, returning them to the land, recreating their world with a perfect city and a renewed temple. In the words of Ezekiel 36, God will gather the people and set them again in their own land, so to glorify the divine name. *Ezekiel 33—48*

It is not ascending real estate values that the prophet promises or the American aspiration for individual privacy symbolized by the white picket fence. Ezekiel envisions that God will provide the most essential *Ezekiel 36:25* signs of lively land: water and a living spirit. On the most basic human level, we need water for survival—the world's poor women walk miles each day to carry the water home. But even where plentiful chlorinated water is only a faucet away, the people seek rivers, lakes, the shore, to immerse themselves in living water. Ezekiel promises that flowing water will be the sign of the new land, clean water sprinkled on all the people. Water will pour out from under the temple and down the streets of the city, turning all the parched dirt paths to rivers of living water. *Ezekiel 47:1–5* Such is the homeland we are promised.

Ezekiel further envisions an infusion of God's spirit. Just as in creation God breathed the divine spirit into Adam, so now again God will breathe life into the whole people. As Ezekiel 37 illustrates this *Ezekiel 36:27* hope, all the dead bones scattered on the dry plain will be infused with *Ezekiel 37:1–10* the breath of God. God will reconnect and energize the bones, the skeletons will grow flesh, the people will live again in their land. The people will rise together and live together in the land, not boxed away in a desperate isolation continually aching for a genuine homeland, but joined together bone to bone praising the *shalom* of God.

Here is one way to envision the resurrection. This is what we gather to celebrate, and Ezekiel recalls to us this divine promise: We shall be given a homeland. All who seek for a home, and that is all the human race, will be given a land and water and a living spirit. The church is a foretaste of this homeland, with its peaceful assemblies and baptismal water enlivened by the spirit of Christ. But the church is only a sign of the promise. God will provide better housing than anything the church and the world can presently contain. The biblical visions become ecstatic, for the prophets try to say what is beyond human language: Our final homeland is at God's right hand. More faltering words! But now we know why all human beings yearn for a home. They yearn for God, for God is our homeland.

THE WORD OF THE LORD came to me: "O human one, when the house of Israel dwelt in their own land, they defiled it by their ways and their doings; their conduct before me was like the uncleanness of one who is impure. So I poured out my wrath upon them for the blood which they had shed in the land, for the idols with which they had defiled it. I scattered them among the nations, and they were dispersed through the countries; in accordance with their conduct and their deeds I judged them. But when they came to the nations, wherever they came, they profaned my holy name, in that it was said of them, 'These are the people of the LORD, and yet they had to go out of the LORD's land.' But I had concern for my holy name, which the house of Israel caused to be profaned among the nations to which they came.

"Therefore say to the house of Israel, Thus says the Lord GOD: It is not for your sake, O house of Israel, that I am about to act, but for the sake of my holy name, which you have profaned among the nations to which you came. And I will vindicate the holiness of my great name, which has been profaned among the nations, and which you have profaned among them; and the nations will know that I am the LORD, says the Lord GOD, when through you I vindicate my holiness before their eyes. For I will take you from the nations, and gather you from all the countries, and bring you into your own land. I will sprinkle clean water upon you, and you shall be clean from all your uncleannesses, and from all your idols I will cleanse you. A new heart I will give you, and a new spirit I will put within you; and I will take out of your flesh the heart of stone and give you a heart of flesh. And I will put my spirit within you, and cause you to walk in my statutes and be careful to observe my ordinances. You shall dwell in the land which I gave to your forebears; and you shall be my people, and I will be your God."

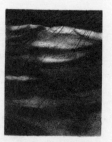

For a peaceful home,
and clear water,
and a lively spirit,
we yearn, O God.
We with housing,
and we without housing,
we yearn, O God,
for the homeland
that is you.

IN 1980 RUSSELL HOBAN, famed for his children's stories of Frances the badger, published *Riddley Walker*, the adventures of a Huck Finn–type boy in the year 2347 OC, "Our Count" being the calendar that emerged sometime after the destruction of our civilization in a nuclear war. Hoban's comic wonder did not receive the readership it deserved, for Riddley's words are cast in the much-altered and bizarrely spelled English of his time. The boy is struggling to discover the meaning of death and life in light of artifacts of our civilization, notably a plaque narrating the legend of St. Eustace found in the ruins of Canterbury Cathedral. In discussing with Riddley this religious shard of our time, the Pry Mincer describes symbol in this way: "Its blipful it aint just only what it seams to be its the syn and foller of some thing else." It ain't just what it seems to be, we say of anything laden with meaning: It both follows and signifies a greater reality. "Its blipful," our word blip having come by Riddley's time to denote import, significance, something extraordinary requiring imaginative consideration.

Russell Hoban, Riddley Walker (New York: Washington Square Press, 1980), 124.

Always More

Sometimes Christians simplistically describe the readings of the Easter Vigil as a walk through the Bible, as if we come annually to a *Reader's Digest* version of the Hebrew Scriptures. But the readings are more blipful than that. They are more than they seem to be, more than a chronological retelling of biblical history. The readings pull us deeper into the meaning of our faith. We immerse ourselves in a river of images: the fire of the gods, the creation of the world, religious sacrifice, the struggle against oppression, the sacred marriage, the primordial flood, the heavenly city, divine wisdom, the dream of the homeland. By claiming these images as our own we join our assembly to the continuous narrative of human religion surprised by divine mercy. We recognize these ancient words as our own story and by God's bounty receive the same amazing grace as did the storytellers we follow.

"Its the syn and foller of some thing else." Not only do the readings tell of the past by following after the encounter with grace: They tell of the future by signifying a gift of grace to come. For the readings also are signs of the Vigil's baptisms. In Genesis 1 God forms the world out of watery chaos; in baptism a new creation is called forth from the watery font. In Genesis 22 the primal religious urge to sacrifice to the gods is circumvented by the baptismal mercy of God. In Exodus 14 the whole people is saved from human misery by crossing together the baptismal sea. Using the images from Isaiah 54 we describe baptism as our marriage with God, our safety after the flood, our peace in the heavenly city. In Isaiah 55 we are served the banquet to which our baptism invites us. In Baruch Lady Wisdom shares her enlightenment with all the baptized, and in Ezekiel 36 the clean water of the perfect homeland is poured on us who assemble here around the font.

"Its the syn and foller of some thing else." Not only do the readings proclaim the grace of baptism: They give us a taste of life in the body of Christ. Genesis 1 offers a communal vision of God's perfect universe, we a part of humanity, and humanity a part of the whole creation. In Genesis 22 we can imagine ourselves to be Abraham and Isaac returning home arm in arm; we are also Sarah, receiving the family back again. In Exodus 14 we are brought together to the safe side of the sea to discover that the shore is only the beginning of centuries of struggle for *shalom*. Isaiah 54 reminds us that the Christian life is not a wedding but a marriage, not the afternoon party but the day-in-day-out years until we die. We are safe in the boat, but there is a storm raging.

Each of us is a building block in the city we seek. The banquet of Isaiah 55 beckons yet more folk to the table, and we are to issue the invitations. Lady Wisdom is no seven-year-old in white ruffles on her first communion day: Lady Wisdom is full of years, the maiden turned crone by decades of righteous living. The homeland of Ezekiel 36, the place of water and the spirit, is not a heavenly rest, but rather the place where we begin our life together.

The annual recitation of these great stories will bring us again not only to witness the baptisms of others, but, as Martin Luther said, to creep back to our own baptism. Continually these narratives and images of our identity call us back to the font and also forward to the community. It's a lot to ask of four or seven or even twelve readings; the task to choose which texts to read from among the dozens of tales of God's mercy is not easy for the lectionary committees laboring over the centuries. How about the story of Hagar's discovery of the well, or *Genesis 21:9–21* Joshua's crossing the Jordan River, or Elijah's summoning the fire of *Joshua 3:7–17* God with prayer and three dousings of water, or Jonah's rescue from the *1 Kings 18:20–39* depths of the sea? Most of our churches not only refer to the flood, but *Genesis 7, 8, 9* read the story of Noah and God's covenant. Several of our churches *Jonah 1—2* not only mention the spirit in Ezekiel, but tell of the vision of the dry bones coming together at the breath of the LORD. *Ezekiel 37:1–14*

One of the stories read in ancient times—and still suggested for Lutheran use, as the night's concluding lesson—is the story from Daniel 3 of the three men in the fiery furnace. Splendidly crafted and with all the repetitions of superb oral storytelling, the tale depicts the faith- *Daniel 3:1–23* ful in the fires of life's furnace. But the faithful are not suffering and dying, for God is in the fire with them. Death has no power over them, says Paul, and we, too, can gaze into the fire of our death rejoic- ing at the empty tomb of Christ. We have died already in baptism, and *Romans 6:1–11* we live in God.

When the evil King Nebuchadnezzar saw the faithful three and a mysterious fourth walking about in the furnace unsinged by the flames, he cried out, "Blessed be the God of Shadrach, Meshach and Abednego! For there is no other god who is able to deliver in this way." Like us, he spoke his words around the fire and praised the God who bears life from death. Like him, we speak our words around the fire, living anew in God, glad to return next year to repeat the words again.

Luke 24:27 When Jesus interpreted his own death to the disciples on the road to Emmaus, he began with the words of Moses and the prophets. The "words of Moses and the prophets" that we read this holy night are illumined by the candle, enacted in the baptisms and realized in the community. These words are much more than we can know, surely much more than any series of meditations can suggest. They are the church's richest fare for hungry hearts, the church's most imaginative images to describe the resurrection. The readings are something like the black lines in the church's coloring book filled in with the mystery of grace. The resurrection, like a flame, is beyond our grasping. But we hold in our hands the ancient stories and poems that praise God's power of life over death, and so we stand together in faith around the fire.

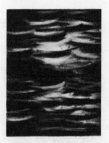

O God, endless grace,
more and more mercy,
say Moses and Miriam,
Huldah and Isaiah,
more and more mercy,
endless grace.

LITERATURE PROFESSORS SOMETIMES ADMIT that if their students haven't the time to read the entire assigned novel, they might get by if they read the first page very carefully. Often the whole book—its themes, its approach, its tone—is on the first page. So it is with the Easter Vigil. If we haven't time in a whole life to ponder all the meanings of all the readings, we can at least learn the chant that is on the first page this night, the Exsultet. For there are varieties of readings, but the same spirit is in them all, and that spirit is revealed in this Easter Proclamation: "This is the night." To see how the Exsultet inserts the readings into the liturgy and so into our liturgical life, it is helpful first to see how it does not.

Let us begin by noting that the vigil is not about that common devotion, pilgrimage. Devout Jews journey to the Wailing Wall, faithful Muslims are urged to visit Mecca, while the Hindu millions wash in the Ganges. It is a common religious idea, that we walk in the steps of the holy ones, that we kiss the place where divinity has stood. When

This Is the Night

in the fourth century Christianity came out of hiding and wealthy people were free to assert their religion publicly, pilgrimage became important also in the church. In medieval Christianity, the common people under the banner of religious war or private penance made pilgrimage to the Holy Land, to walk where Jesus had walked.

In religious pilgrimage, a time back then is revered as holier than this time. We remember a savior or a holy people who lived in the past. For some religions, the precise historical dates of revelations are significant, and by devout attention to the holy past the believers come close to God. Some of this search for the sacred past has come into Christian Holy Week observances. Some try to export the Holy Land by building replicas of shrines. Some try to make of Holy Week a kind of Oberammergau, in which dramatic representation returns us to the passion of Christ.

The Easter Vigil will never fit this description. The liturgy does not try to beam us back to the environs of Jerusalem, so that we can be around to glimpse the angels' descent at Easter dawn. We do not speculate on the feelings of the holy women. The Vigil proposes not memory, but metaphor; not pilgrimage, but liturgy. When the fourteenth-century mystic, Margery Kempe, became hysterical with weeping while gazing at a statue of the Pieta, an annoyed priest said to her, "Woman, Jesus is long since dead." But she answered, "Sir, his death is as fresh to me as if he had died this same day, and so, I think, it ought to be to you and to all Christian people." Kempe was not on pilgrimage to the Holy Land when this occurred, but was in Norwich, England, at St. Stephen Church. She was responding to an image of salvation alive to her in a local church. "As if he had died this same day," Kempe says. "This is the night," the Exsultet says, still more emphatically.

The Book of Margery Kemp (trans., B.A. Windead) (New York: Penguin Books 1985), 18.

To be sure, the Exsultet presents images from the history of salvation. The proclamation recalls the debt of Adam, the blood of sacrifice, the escape from Egypt and the crossing of the sea. But these events did not take place in a time back then. The creation of light in Genesis 1, banishing the ancient darkness, is praised in this single candle. We recall not the women waiting at the tomb; rather we laud the exodus as a metaphor for this present night. "This is the night," the chant proclaims. Here is God's glory, in this candle. Here is God's might, in this assembly. Here is God's mercy, in this font, this meal, this community. And it is not easy for us to believe this. Religion typically reverences the bones of the martyrs. The Exsultet suggests that we reverence also the assembly, for *this* is the night, *this* is the people who are saved.

"This is the night" is the Christian translation of the question that the youngest child asks at the Jewish seder: "Why is this night different from all other nights?" The answer in our passover ritual is that tonight the people gathered around this fire and book and font and table are crossing the sea. We mark the paschal candle both with the alphabetical signs of Christ—the alpha and the omega—and with this year's date. The year of the crucifixion matters nothing. *This* is the night: The beginning and the end meet in the present.

The Exsultet concludes with a plea that when Christ comes, this candle still will be burning. This candle, a small light in the morning of our paschal liturgy, awaits Christ the Morning Star, that preeminent light transforming all the world's present darkness. Our words, and the words of centuries of the faithful before us, keep vigil through the waiting years by dancing around the fire of this Morning Star, which flickers and blazes, bursts and explodes in our midst. And we say: Surely the fire of God will come to purify the creation; surely the light of God will illumine the present darkness. And we pray: Come, Morning Star, not as the tiny glow we see in the dimmest distance, but as a magnificent burning divine might that, were we close by, could sear our eyesight with the brilliance of mercy. Around the fire we pray: Come, shining Spirit, and kindle in us the fire of your love.